W9-DIE-735

THE LITTLE BROWN BEAN BOOK

A lively and informative introduction to the delicious world of beans.

THE LITTLE BROWN BEAN BOOK

by

David Eno

Illustrated by Clive Birch

THORSONS PUBLISHERS LIMITED
Wellingborough, Northamptonshire

This enlarged, revised and reset edition first published
1983
Second Impression 1984

© THORSONS PUBLISHERS LTD 1983

British Library Cataloguing in Publication Data

Eno, David
    The little brown bean book.
    1. Cookery (Beans)
    I. Title
    641.6'565   TX803.B4

    ISBN 0-7225-0848-4

Printed and bound in Great Britain

CONTENTS

INTRODUCTION

Pulses can be a most useful addition to the diet providing a variety of cheap nutritious dishes.

Unlike most other high protein foods they can be stored for long periods without deterioration. Another advantage is that they are comparatively cheap and can even be grown in one's own garden.

The unusually high protein content of pulses is explained by the fact that the leguminous plants which produce them share a remarkable symbiotic relationship with certain nitrogen fixing bacteria which inhabit their roots and which are able to make nitrogen available to them. All plants require nitrogen to manufacture proteins which are as vital to them as they are to us. While most other plants rely on nitrogen compounds being present in the soil, leguminous plants have access to the unfailing supplies from the air and consequently manufacture and store large amounts of protein, particularly in their seeds.

While it is true that many pulses do not contain the exact balance of amino acids (the components of protein) required in human nutrition, the missing or inadequate amino acids are readily supplied by other foods and these can be combined into the same dish or eaten during the same meal. In this way a complete balance of amino acids may be assimilated. However soya beans and mung beans with 61 per cent and 57 per cent protein which is immediately usable by the body closely approach meat which has an average value of 67 per cent so can be used as direct substitutes.

Although specific pulses are suggested in most of the recipes do not be afraid to experiment and substitute others in their place. Don't forget also that cooking times may need to be adjusted.

SOAKING

All pulses should first be washed in a colander or strainer. They are frequently dusty and lentils in particular often have small stones mixed with them. Pick out any that are bad or discoloured.

Most pulses require soaking for at least 12 hours and preferably for 24. You may find it easier to put several batches of pulses in to soak at the same time, storing those you don't need in the fridge where they will keep for about five days. Lentils, split peas, aduki beans and black-eyed beans can be cooked without prior soaking. During soaking most pulses double their size, but soya beans increase by three times.

COOKING

Pulses should be cooked in the same water as that in which they were soaked so as to retain minerals, vitamins and flavour. Salt should never be added until cooking is finished as this retards the softening process. Thorough cooking until completely soft is essential for palatability and ease of digestion. It is a good idea to cook pulses well in advance of a meal to ensure enough time can be allowed for this purpose. It is difficult to give precise cooking times, although they are indicated in the recipes, as they tend to vary with age and storage conditions. Where possible it is best to cook pulses separately from other vegetables.

A pressure cooker is particularly useful with pulses which take a long time to cook, such as soya beans and chick peas, and can reduce the time required by about two-thirds. Excellent stews can also be quickly made in a pressure cooker. Another way to speed up cooking is to grind pulses to flour in a coffee or grain mill. This does away with the need for soaking and enables cooking to be completed in 15 to 20 minutes. Ready ground soya beans in the form of soya flour can be bought in most health and wholefood stores. This is an extremely useful additive which can be used for enriching bread, cakes, muesli and savory dishes.

When a purée is required this can be made either

in a liquidizer, a hand soup blender, or by passing through a sieve.

A large gravy strainer is also ideal together with a wooden spoon which is used for rubbing the pulp through. This process is much easier if the pulses are still hot from cooking.

CLIVE BIRCH

SEASONING

Whereas freshly picked peas and beans are full of their own flavour and need little treatment apart from light steaming or boiling, dried pulses tend to be bland and require a bold hand with the seasoning to counteract this. Herbs, onions, garlic, and tomatoes blend particularly well with pulses and can be used to intensify flavour together with freshly ground black pepper and sea salt.

SPROUTING BEANS

The beansprouts which are now on sale in many supermarkets and greengrocers shops are grown from mung beans. These are small green beans which are traditional in Chinese cookery. All beans and many seeds can be sprouted with equal success, and several seed companies now sell packets of various seeds specifically for this purpose. The resulting sprouts are sweet and crunchy and highly nutritious. Sprouted beans and grains contain a large proportion of vitamins and are a delicious addition to salads and fried rice dishes. Suitable candidates include: red beans, soya beans, black-eyed beans, chick peas, wheat and grains.

Although special plastic sprouters are available, and make sprouting almost foolproof, with a little more perseverance a jam jar (preferably two pound size) can be used with equal success. The beans are first soaked overnight and next morning the water is poured away. At this stage it is easiest to fix a piece of muslin across the top of the jar with a rubber band. Keep the sprouts in a warm place, light is not necessary. Wash morning and night by filling the jar with cold water through the muslin and then inverting for a few minutes. When the sprouts have grown to three times the length of the original seed they are ready. This normally takes three to five days.

The sprouts can be used in a number of ways — raw in salads and sandwiches, or lightly cooked in rice dishes, soups, curries, etc.

Note: Many of the recipes in this book use *pre-cooked* beans, please check each recipe carefully to make sure you have pre-cooked beans where necessary.

SOUPS AND STARTERS

LENTIL SOUP

1 small onion
1 tomato
1 clove garlic
2 tablespoonsful vegetable oil
1½ pints (¾ litre) vegetable stock or water
½ cupful red lentils
1 stick celery with leaves
2 tablespoonsful chopped parsley

1. Slice and fry the onion, peeled tomato and garlic in the vegetable oil and when soft add the stock and lentils.

2. Chop the celery finely including the leaves and add to the soup with the parsley, salt and pepper.

3. Bring to the boil and simmer very gently for 20 minutes.

4. Place in a liquidizer and blend for 2 minutes or pass through a sieve.

Serves 4.

PEA SOUP

½ lb (¼ kilo) dried peas, soaked
2 pints (1 litre) vegetable stock
1 large onion
3 sticks celery
2 leeks
1 carrot
1 potato
2 oz (50g) butter
Sea salt and ground pepper

1. Cook the soaked peas in the vegetable stock until soft, which should take between 1 and 2 hours or in a pressure cooker for about 30 minutes.

2. *Sauté* the onion and leeks in the butter and when cooked add ½ pint (¼ litre) of stock and the other vegetables chopped or diced.

3. Cook for 20 minutes and then add to the peas when they are ready.

4. Cook for a further 30 minutes over a very low heat and then pass through a sieve and season to taste.'

Note: The same soup made with chick peas is delicious.

Serves 4 to 5.

SOYA BEAN SOUP

A quickly made and nutritious soup.

1 onion
2 tomatoes, skinned
3 tablespoonsful vegetable oil
4 tablespoonsful soya flour
2 tablespoonsful wholemeal flour
1½ pints (¾ litre) vegetable stock or water
1½ teaspoonsful yeast extract
Sea salt and ground pepper to taste

1. Chop the onion and skinned tomatoes finely and *sauté* in the oil in a large pan.

2. When they are well cooked stir in the soya flour and wheat flour and cook for a few minutes longer.

3. Add the stock gradually, stirring continuously to avoid lumps. When all the stock is added bring to the boil, add the yeast extract, and simmer for 15 minutes.

4. Season with salt and pepper and any fresh chopped herbs you wish.

5. If you prefer a completely smooth soup pass it through a sieve.

Serves 4.

RED BEAN PÂTÉ

This pâté, better than any made with meat, can be eaten on biscuits, melba toast, toasted pitta bread, etc.

1 medium onion
2 oz (50g) butter
4 oz (100g) mushrooms
2 large sticks celery
2 cloves garlic
2 cupsful red kidney beans, pre-cooked
2 tablespoonsful parsley, chopped
4 oz (100g) black olives
1 tablespoonful tomato purée
2 teaspoonsful yeast extract
Sea salt
Freshly ground pepper

1. Fry the sliced onion in the butter and after 5 minutes add the chopped mushrooms, chopped celery and pulped garlic.

2. Add the pre-cooked beans with any juice left from cooking and simmer for 25 minutes in a pan with a lid.

3. Chop the parsley and prepare the olives by stoning and chopping finely.

4. Whilst the bean mixture is still hot sieve or

liquidize and stir in the rest of the ingredients.

5. Spoon into a suitable dish for serving. As the pâté cools it will thicken, and should be refrigerated for at least an hour before serving.

SNACKS

BAKED BEANS

---

1 onion
2 tablespoonsful vegetable oil
½ lb (¼ kilo) tomatoes
¾ lb (350g) soaked haricot beans
1 cupful soaking water from the above
¼ teaspoonful curry powder
1-2 teaspoonsful soft raw cane sugar
½ teaspoonful sea salt
¼ teaspoonful ground ginger

1. *Sauté* the finely chopped onion in the oil in a casserole.

2. Add the peeled, sliced tomatoes, and the rest of the ingredients.

3. Cook in a slow oven 250°F/130°C (Gas Mark ½) for 3 hours or until the beans are cooked. Check occasionally that there is enough liquid and top up with water if necessary.

4. Serve with toasted and buttered wholemeal bread.

Serves 4.

HUMMUS

This is a sensational dip or spread which you just can't stop eating.

½ lb (¼ kilo) chick peas
Juice of 1 lemon
¼ pint (150ml) vegetable oil
2 cloves garlic, pulped
4 tablespoonsful tahini
Sea salt
Chopped mint

1. Soak the chick peas for 24 hours then cook until soft which will take at least three hours or in a pressure cooker one hour. When the peas are really soft strain them but save the liquid.

2. Put in a liquidizer and blend to a smooth paste adding the lemon juice and some of the water if the mixture begins to clog.

3. Add the oil, garlic, tahini and salt to taste, then turn into a serving bowl. Stir in or sprinkle with chopped mint.

4. Alternatively, some of the cooked chick peas can be saved, deep fried and used to decorate the top.

SAVOURY LENTILS

1 cupful green or brown lentils
1 pint (½ litre) vegetable stock (or 1 pint (½ litre) water with 1 tablespoonful yeast extract)
1 onion
Vegetable oil
1 tablespoonful wholemeal flour
Juice of 1 lemon

1. Soak the lentils overnight in the vegetable stock. Cook in the same stock for 30 minutes or until soft, adding water during cooking if required.

2. *Sauté* the onion in the oil.

3. When the lentils are done drain them well in a colander and then stir in the flour. Mix the lentils with the *sautéed* onion, dress with the lemon juice, and serve.

Serves 4.

BEAN BURGERS

These burgers can be substituted for the meaty variety and make delicious hamburgers with wholemeal rolls and fried onions, or can be eaten hot or cold with salads or in sandwiches.

> ½ lb (¼ kilo) red kidney beans, soaked
> 2 large onions
> 1½ oz (40g) butter
> 4 tablespoonsful parsley, chopped
> 2 oz (50g) wholemeal flour
> 2 oz (50g) wholemeal breadcrumbs
> 1 tablespoonful tamari
> 1 tablespoonful tomato purée

1. Leave the beans to soak overnight. Next day boil in a large pan with plenty of water (and no salt).

2. While the beans are cooking *sauté* the onion in the butter until soft.

3. When the beans are cooked, which will take at least 30 minutes, strain in a colander and then mash. Stir in the cooked onions and the rest of the ingredients and leave to cool.

4. Roll out on a floured board and cut into rounds with a large tumbler or biscuit cutter.

5. Fry in shallow oil until crisp on both sides and serve.

SALADS

Fresh peas and beans can be useful in salads both raw and cooked while cooked dried beans can be used in a number of ways.

CLIVE BIRCH

RED KIDNEY BEAN SALAD

1 clove garlic
1 lettuce
2 tablespoonsful French dressing
1 cupful cooked red kidney beans
1 tablespoonful chopped chives

1. Prepare a salad bowl by rubbing the inside with the garlic.

2. Wash and drain the lettuce thoroughly. Chop it coarsely and mix with the dressing, beans and chopped chives in the bowl.

CHICK PEA MAYONNAISE

1 cupful chick peas, cooked
1 tablespoonful, chopped parsley
½ cupful garlic mayonnaise
Paprika

Mix the ingredients and sprinkle with paprika.

MIXED BEAN AND ONION SALAD

2 cupsful cooked beans
1 small onion
2 tablespoonsful French dressing

1. Select two types of bean which cook in approximately the same time, e.g., aduki and black-eyed.

2. Mix with the finely shredded onion and toss in French dressing.

BUTTER BEAN AND HERB SALAD

1 cupful butter beans, pre-cooked
1 lettuce
2 tablespoonsful parsley, chopped
2 tablespoonsful chives, chopped
2 tablespoonsful chervil, chopped
¼ cupful French dressing

1. Drain the cooked butter beans.

2. Wash and dry the lettuce and shred with a sharp knife.

3. Chop the herbs and mix the ingredients together, stirring to distribute them thoroughly.

LENTIL AND TOMATO SALAD

½ lb (¼ kilo) green or brown lentils, soaked
4 tablespoonsful tomato juice
1 tablespoonful lemon juice
1 clove garlic, crushed
2 tablespoonsful olive oil
Sea salt
Freshly ground pepper
4 spring onions
4 tomatoes
2 sticks celery
2 tablespoonsful parsley, chopped

1. Drain the soaked lentils, add fresh cold water and cook for 30 to 40 minutes until they are soft but still intact. Drain in a colander and allow to cool. Turn into a large mixing bowl.

2. Prepare a dressing by mixing the tomato juice, lemon juice, crushed garlic, olive oil and seasoning.

3. Chop the spring onions, tomato and celery.

4. Put all the ingredients into the mixing bowl with the lentils. Add the dressing and turn thoroughly but gently until all the ingredients are mixed. Turn into a salad bowl and serve.

MAIN MEALS

BAKED LENTIL PIE

¾ lb (350g) lentils (of any type)
½ lb (½ kilo) potatoes
½ oz (15g) of butter
Milk
Sea salt and freshly ground pepper
1 onion
1 lb (½ kilo) tomatoes
4 tablespoonsful vegetable oil
1 bay leaf

1. Cook the soaked lentils until soft and strain off any excess water.

2. Boil the potatoes and, when cooked, mash with butter, a little milk, salt and pepper.

3. Gently cook the chopped onion and peeled sliced tomatoes in the vegetable oil until soft.

4. Put the lentils in the bottom of a well greased casserole and add the onions, tomatoes and bay leaf. For the final layer spread over with the mashed potato.

5. Bake for 30 minutes at 375°F/190°C (Gas Mark 5) and serve with lightly steamed green vegetables.

Serves 4.

BEAN CURRY

*2 cupsful brown rice for serving with the
curry
2 onions
2-3 cloves garlic
Vegetable oil
2 large cooking apples
½ pint (¼ litre) vegetable stock
3 carrots
¼ lb (250g) mushrooms
1-3 teaspoonful curry powder
2 cupsful cooked beans
1 teaspoonful yeast extract
1-2 teaspoonful soft raw cane sugar
Sea salt to taste*

1. Put the rice on to cook while the curry is
   being prepared.

2. *Sauté* the chopped onions and crushed garlic
   in the oil and when they are soft add the
   peeled, cored and sliced apples.

3. Continue to cook over a low heat until the
   apple softens and then add the stock, the
   diced carrots, mushrooms, and the rest of
   the ingredients. (Unless you are experienced
   with the particular curry powder you are
   using it is best to go carefully at first, adding

just a little and testing its effect.)

4. Bring to the boil and then simmer over a very low heat. After 30 minutes of cooking add the beans and cooked potato and simmer for a further 20 minutes or longer. (The flavour of the curry is much improved by long and gentle cooking. Also by using a heavy iron pan with a heat diffuser beneath it.) Keep the lid on all the time. Serve with the rice.

Serves 4.

DAHL

This is an excellent dish to accompany a curry and is always much appreciated. This recipe differs from the traditional Indian version.

> ½ lb (¼ kilo) red lentils
> 1 onion
> 2-3 cloves of garlic
> 1 tablespoonful of vegetable oil or butter
> 1 lb (½ kilo) fresh tomatoes or 1 tin
> 1 oz (25g) butter
> Sea salt

1. Wash the lentils and cook with three times their volume of cold water (no soaking is necessary).

2. Prepare a tomato sauce by frying the chopped onion and garlic in the oil, then add the peeled tomato and simmer for 20 minutes.

3. When the lentils are cooked they should have absorbed most of the water. The tomato sauce should have thickened somewhat so that when the two are added together with the butter the resulting mixture has a fairly thick consistency and is definitely not runny.

4.   Season with salt to taste.

Note: The result should have an intense flavour and if you feel it is not strong enough add a little tomato *purée* and some more garlic.

SPAGHETTI WITH ADUKI BEANS

This is spaghetti served with a basic tomato sauce. The beans add flavour and protein and make it into a satisfying meal. The aim is to have the pasta and sauce ready at the same time. Whilst the sauce will lose nothing from cooling and re-heating, the pasta should be served the minute it is cooked. These quantities are sufficient for 3 to 4 servings.

The Sauce:

> 1 medium onion
> 2 tablespoonsful good quality vegetable oil
> 2 cloves garlic
> 2 lb (1 kilo) ripe tomatoes or 1 large tin preserved
> Tomato purée (optional)
> 1 cupful aduki beans, pre-cooked

1. Peel and slice the onions thinly and fry in a pan with the oil. Add the sliced or crushed garlic.

2. Skin the tomatoes, dipping first in boiling water for a few seconds, and add to the pan. (Fresh tomatoes can be replaced by preserved when out of season or if too expensive. With either fresh or preserved tomatoes a teaspoonful or so of tomato *purée* may also be needed depending on their flavour.)

36

3. After about 10 minutes of cooking add the pre-cooked aduki beans. Continue cooking gently until some of the juice has been driven off and the sauce thickens. This should take 15 to 25 minutes.

4. Season with sea salt and freshly ground pepper.

The Pasta:

> 1 lb (½ kilo) pasta (3 oz/75g-4 oz/100g per person)
> 1 clove garlic
> 1 oz (25g) butter
> 4 tablespoonsful chopped parsley
> 2 oz (50g) Cheddar cheese, finely grated

1. Bring a large pan of salted water to the boil then add the pasta, stirring frequently with a wooden spoon to prevent the pasta sticking to itself, and the pan. Cooking will take from 15 to 25 minutes, depending on the type of pasta. This period should leave it cooked all the way through, but firm, and definitely not soggy. When ready turn into a colander and leave to drain thoroughly for at least 2 minutes.

2. Prepare a serving bowl by rubbing with half a clove of garlic and adding a knob of butter.

The bowl *must* be warmed in a low oven which will also melt the butter.

3. Transfer the pasta and stir in the chopped parsley and grated cheese.

4. The bean or tomato sauce may now be added or served at the table in a separate dish.

BEANS WITH COURGETTES

This dish is simplicity itself to prepare. The beans must be well cooked but not mushy.

3 tablespoonsful vegetable oil
1 large onion
2 cloves garlic
1 green pepper
2 cupsful cooked haricot or soya beans
1 lb (½ kilo) tomatoes
1 lb (½ kilo) courgettes
Freshly ground sea salt and pepper
½ teaspoonful oregano

1. Put the vegetable oil in a heavy pan over a low heat.

2. Chop the onion, garlic, and pepper and put into the pan. Add the beans, the peeled sliced tomatoes and the sliced courgettes. Season with a little salt and pepper and add the oregano.

3. With a closely fitting lid on the pan allow to cook very gently for half an hour. Alternatively, place in a casserole in a moderate oven for half an hour or until the vegetables are cooked.

4. Serve with brown rice.

Serves 4.

MIXED BEAN STEW

The times indicated are suitable for any bean which cooks fairly quickly, for example, aduki beans, brown lentils, black-eyed beans, split peas, red kidney beans, butter beans, pinto beans, bolotti beans, all of which must have been soaked beforehand.

1 large onion
2 cloves garlic
4 oz (100g) mushrooms
Vegetable oil
2 pints (1 litre) vegetable stock
4 oz (100g) mixed beans
3 large carrots
3 large potatoes
½ small swede
2 Jerusalem artichokes (optional)
2 teaspoonsful yeast extract
1 teaspoonful chopped thyme
Sea salt and freshly ground pepper to taste
1 tablespoonful cornflour

1. *Sauté* the chopped onion, garlic and mushrooms in the oil and when cooked add the vegetable stock and the soaked beans. Cook for 35 minutes.

2. Add the prepared and diced vegetables and

40

other ingredients except for the cornflour. Cook for another 35 minutes or until the vegetables and beans are done.

3. Add any further seasoning that may be required and thicken with the cornflour, first mixing the powder with a little of the liquid from the stew in a cup. When it is lump free mix into the stew and bring to the boil stirring until thickening has occurred.

4. Reduce the times by at least half when using a pressure cooker.

Serves 4.

RED HOT BEANS!

This is a meatless version of Chilli con Carne.

> *¾ lb (350g) red kidney beans*
> *2 onions*
> *Vegetable oil*
> *2-3 large aubergines, diced*
> *1 lb (½ kilo) tomatoes*
> *Sea salt and freshly ground pepper to taste*
> *2 cloves garlic*
> *Chilli powder*
> *1 teaspoonful ground coriander*

1. Soak the beans overnight and cook for 1½ hours or half an hour in a pressure cooker.

2. Fry the onions in a heavy iron pan and when soft add the diced aubergine. (These will soak up the oil, so keep adding more as they do so.)

3. When the aubergines are soft add the tomatoes, salt, pepper, garlic and spices, starting with a very small amount of chilli powder, enough to cover the tip of a knife.

4. After 15 minutes cooking add the cooked beans and simmer for a further half an hour over a very gentle heat. Add more chilli powder to taste, but be careful as there is

nothing you can do if too much is added, except sweat it out!

5.   Serve with brown rice.

Serves 4.

LENTIL ROAST

The mixture described below may either be roasted in an oven-proof dish or used to form rissoles which can be fried. Any type of cooked bean may be substituted for the lentils.

> ½ lb (¼ kilo) red lentils
> 2 onions, chopped
> 1 clove garlic, chopped
> Vegetable oil
> 2 cupsful wholemeal breadcrumbs
> 1 teaspoonful each of chopped sage, thyme, parsley
> Sea salt and freshly ground pepper
> 2 eggs
> 4 oz (100g) grated Cheddar cheese

1. Cook the lentils in three times their own volume of water, which should take about 15 minutes.

2. Fry the chopped onion and garlic in the oil and when cooked add to the breadcrumbs in a mixing bowl.

3. Add the chopped herbs, salt and pepper, then mix.

4. Finally add the eggs and the cooked lentils and mix thoroughly.

5. Place in a well greased tin sprinkle with cheese and cook in a cool oven, 325°F/170°C (Gas Mark 3) for 40 minutes or until firm.

Note: Good served with roast potatoes and green vegetables, or can be left to cool and served in slices. Cold leftover slices can be fried.

Serves 6.

SOYA BEAN AND LEEK QUICHE

6 oz (150g) of wholemeal short crust pastry
1 onion
2 large leeks
Vegetable oil
1 cupful cooked soya beans
2 large eggs
½ pint (¼ litre) milk (up to ¼ pint (150ml)
milk can be replaced by single cream)
Sea salt and freshly ground pepper
1 tablespoonful chopped parsley
1 teaspoonful chopped thyme
2 oz (50g) grated Cheddar cheese

1. Line a large flan tin with the pastry. Prick the bottom all over with a fork and bake blind in a pre-heated oven at 350°F/180°C (Gas Mark 4) for 15 minutes.

2. Cook the finely chopped onions and leeks in the oil over a low heat in a covered pan. When soft turn the leeks into the flan case and sprinkle with the soya beans.

3. Beat the eggs with the milk, salt, pepper and herbs and then pour over the leeks and beans.

4. Grate the cheese over the top and cook for 20 to 30 minutes at 375°F/190°C (Gas Mark

5) when the centre should have set.

Note: This is equally good served with a salad, or with cooked vegetables such as sprouting broccoli, asparagus, kale, new potatoes, etc.

BUTTER BEAN ROAST

½ lb (¼ kilo) butter beans
3 onions
4 oz (100g) mushrooms
Vegetable oil
4 oz (100g) vegetable rissole mix
1 egg, beaten
1 tablespoonful parsley, chopped
1 teaspoonful sage, chopped
Sea salt
Freshly ground black pepper

1. Soak the beans overnight and next day cook until soft in the same water, adding more water if needed. When the beans are ready mash thoroughly.

2. Finely slice the onions and mushrooms and *sauté* them in the oil over a gentle heat for about 20 minutes.

3. Mix the vegetable rissole mix with the recommended amount of water and then add the other ingredients including the mashed beans.

4. Place in a greased baking tin and bake at 375°F/190°C (Gas Mark 5) for 30 minutes or until browned on top.

FRESH PEAS AND BEANS

COOKING

Although peas and beans are most often cooked they can be delicious eaten raw in salads. However, the older they are the less palatable they become and so cooking may be necessary. To get the best possible flavour and texture light cooking only should be given.

Steaming is by far the best method and young peas and broad beans should be given 5 to 10 minutes while French beans, Mangetout and runner beans should be given up to 15 minutes. A sprig of mint can be added during cooking.

The simplest way to serve is to toss in butter and sprinkle with sea salt, and this is probably best if you are planning to have a complicated main dish. However, if you wish to serve them in a more elaborate way, here are some suggestions.

BEANS WITH TOMATO SAUCE

This recipe is applicable to French or green beans, young broad beans still in their pods, or hulled broad beans.

> *1 lb (½ kilo) beans*
> *1 lb (½ kilo) fresh tomatoes or 1 tin*
> *1 clove garlic*
> *1 tablespoonful vegetable oil*
> *1 oz (25g) butter*
> *1 teaspoonful honey*
> *½ teaspoonful finely chopped thyme*
> *Sea salt*

1. *Sauté* the sliced or crushed garlic in the oil in a saucepan until it begins to brown.

2. Add the peeled sliced tomatoes and cook gently over a low heat for 15 minutes adding the thyme towards the end. Season with pepper and salt and add the honey.

3. Prepare and steam the beans. When they are ready drain off the water and toss the beans in butter in the pan.

4. Pour over the tomato sauce which may first be sieved or liquidized, and serve immediately.

Serves 4.

GREEN OR FRENCH BEANS WITH CHEESE

1 lb (½ kilo) beans
4 oz (100g) grated Cheddar cheese
½ clove garlic
1 oz (25g) butter
Sea salt

1. The beans should be prepared, cut into short lengths and steamed.

2. Prepare a mixture of the melted butter, crushed garlic and a little salt on a plate.

3. When the beans are done throw away the water and toss the beans in the butter mixture.

4. Sprinkle over the cheese and stir to distribute it evenly. Serve immediately.

Enough for 4.

PEAS AND BEANS WITH GARLIC
MAYONNAISE OR FRENCH DRESSING

Cooked peas and beans are delicious with garlic
mayonnaise either hot or cold as a side dish. Cold
cooked beans can be mixed with French dressing.

BROAD BEAN SALAD

1 lb (½ kilo) broad beans, freshly shelled or frozen
2 tablespoonsful lemon juice
1 teaspoonful salad oil
3 tablespoonsful natural yogurt
4 tablespoonsful garlic mayonnaise
1 tablespoonful chopped parsley
1 tablespoonful choppd chives

1. Boil the beans in salted water for 10 minutes, or if frozen follow the instructions.

2. Drain in a colander and leave to cool.

3. Dress with the lemon juice and oil and turn into a salad bowl.

4. Mix the yogurt, mayonnaise and chopped herbs, pour over the beans, and serve.

INDEX